OTI BAJE

OTI BAJE

MOORE

TUN SHE

- (there is) **DISLOCATION- FIX IT**

[*Ya lalashe - JARA*]   [Omebia la - OMIE SIA]

XULON PRESS ELITE

Xulon Press Elite
2301 Lucien Way #415
Maitland, FL 32751
407.339.4217
www.xulonpress.com

Unless otherwise indicated, Scripture quotations taken from the King James Version (KJV)—*public domain*.

Edited by Xulon Press.

Printed in the United States of America.

ISBN-13: 978-1-54565-533-7

Dedication

To Honorable Dele Babatunde: President, Student Union University of Ife, Ile-Ife, Nigeria

Introduction

What was the world like when there was no government of any kind, someone might inquire? However, another equally competing question could be, was there a time that people of the world actually lacked a governmental structure of one kind or another? What is government, of what significance is it, and how have the various people of the world been governed over the years?

Governments (democracies) give service to the people, including providing amenities to the people, sanctioning and/or punishing offenders, and also protecting the people from external aggression. Yet what did Adam and Eve do as first governor and deputy governor when a capital crime was committed in their world—murder! (I am sure most of their daughters were crying and a few—maybe one or two—said good for him; he was not going to marry any of us, even if he didn't die; that holy guy was always meditating and ready to go to heaven before God really called him up [to those that may wonder, incest was not a sin very early in human history]). We are talking about democracy, and whereas the United States has the most sophisticated democracy in the whole world, hers is neither the largest nor the first The first was Athens: 508 BC—508 BC and the largest today is India.

Should the question be asked, what is the most important thing in electioneering campaigns? We may have different answers from voters and candidates alike: some voters may only enjoy the amusements of the campaign—which occurred to this writer in his first year at the university. On the other hand, we would have the same answer from the contestants, which is to win the election. In addition, this should be the prime concern of the electorate, the citizen voters, who ought to be all eligible citizens eighteen years and older. However, unfortunately I know some good people who care not a hoot about electioneering campaign, they don't care about who wins or who loses, and they don't even enjoy the amusement that goes along with campaigns. These disaffected voters threw this writer into the political arena, which he has remained in for a long, long time!

What is this thing called politics really about? Some call it a game—albeit a dirty game. What is politics made of and how may it be played, and are there examples through history that help? A name that quickly comes to mind is Winston Churchill. I am sure one can always think about one or more names, but this man stands apart and shoulder high. Another name that quickly comes to mind is Mahatma Gandhi. Do we add Obafemi Awolowo to the list? Maybe we shouldn't because he became neither prime minister nor president like those previously mentioned, yet no less a man as rebel leader Chukwuemeka Odumegwu Ojukwu called him—*the best president Nigeria never had*. Even though I disagreed with him completely in his unpatriotic secessionist drive, I do agree with him completely in this—whatever may be at the back of his mind when he made that statement at the passing to the world beyond of the sage Obafemi Awolowo. There is a superior advantage available only to the citizen-voter that is not available to all others anywhere of determining who wins the election and by default those that are defeated!

Contents

0.
Preamble

While democracy and the electioneering campaigning are unique to this field, its principle could easily be applied to any other area of life and living, such as contract negotiations in business, love and romance, or even regarding the survival or imminent extinction of a race. I suppose it is also useful in diplomacy and in international relations; the list goes on. Did Absalom use democracy to try and become the next president and or king of Israel while his father was still alive? I think so. President or king, I said, but alas, even until now Israel has no president, for God is their president. Instead they have a prime minister just like Britain which has both prime minister and king or queen. Yes, Israel had a king for a while, but then many—or some felt—it was wrong, and it stopped. Another good example is General Ibrahim Babangida, who really wasn't a president or a king but more of a military dictator, and when there was agitation for him to leave office, he set up an interim government with a president who was overthrown by the head of the army of that interim government, General Sani Abacha, who now called himself president. However one might say he was a military president because there was no election with voters choosing him to be the next president.

What really is the advantage of a democratically elected government or president, and what is required of him to usher in a better society? Will there ever be a sincere politician, some may ask, but I think the question ought to be reframed to read, will sincere politicians be the norm in our world at any time or just these crooked and good-for-nothing sycophants?

1.
Uniqueness of Democratic Politicking

Politicking and campaigning are carried out in specific standard ways with just one purpose in mind although it has several ramifications and diversifications. No matter how different the situations may be, the frameworks are all the same: to confuse, deceive, or bamboozle, with the intention to sell a product, service, or person to the seller's advantage. Yes, the buyer too may be advantaged, but this is not the primary motive of most, if not all, politicians. But what about Indira Gandhi, some might ask. I mention that lady, in error instead of the man who bore the same surname with her: Mahatma Gandhi but much earlier than her and mistakenly called her father: Jawaharlal Nehru, who too was in politics and so ruled India also. Gandhi Senior was the leader of the Indian independence movement against the British, and he employed nonviolent civil disobedience that the American sage Dr. Martin Luther King Jr. took after. He led India to independence and it is a known fact that he inspired movements for civil rights and movement across the world. He lived modestly, not extravagantly, like many modern-day politicians. He was also said to have undertaken long fasts for self-purification and political protests. Which of our present-day politicians can or would do that? Two things about him are worthy of note for which one of the fathers of Nigeria (on the back cover of this book) is like him: he was a lawyer and was also imprisoned for a long time! Unfortunately, though, he was assassinated on January 30, 1948, in New Delhi, India.

Earlier it was said in this chapter that there is one purpose in mind in the aspects of politics this book is about, which is winning at all costs, but Gandhi stood out. His life's ambition was service and not to take undue advantage of his position as many appear to be doing today, I dare say, in the whole wide world. So whereas winning is all important to candidates, it would be worth the trouble to consider the service you will want to render when you are elected before being elected or else you will just drift away like a particle in the tide with all that will be happening to you—almost, it could be said, bombarding you while in office. I just wish I could go more into this, but this is not the purpose of this book apart from the fact that there are specialized others who handle this: advisers, they are called, I think.

And by the way, politicking campaigns and elections do not last long at all. However, the period is intense and the help of all is needed if *democracy is a government of the people by the people and for the people*. Yes, some make their wealth at this time, but if I have a say, it shouldn't be so at all. I certainly do not refer to advertising or other aspects of marketing and management services, which should be paid for especially where the candidate lacks that expertise, but can the charges not be reduced? But really, there are things that should be done very willingly and free for candidates. The most crucial is the ninety days allowed for candidates to collect signatures to get on the ballot. I mean independent candidates, for many more others attempt to get on the ballot via party primaries. I also would love it if questions were minimized or abstained from completely; just sign the petition sheet and move on. But certainly wait for that candidate after that ninety-days' period when the endorser then determines if (s)he will vote for that candidate endorsed or for a better and more suitable candidate, given their positions and campaigns. I especially appeal for assistance to independent candidates to get on the ballot in this regard as they have a much more uphill task to overcome. My appeal here is that the electorate should budget some time for the campaigns and election day beginning with the endorsement period. After all we do not have elections every year but only every four years. Let us make ours a true democracy, that the triumphant candidate is truly the people's choice not choice via any other variable such as bias, money, or discrimination (tribalism in the Third World), to mention just three factors.

I also think this process and segment of politics has some healing virtues for the general public though some feel real pain after, as one candidate said on TV a little over a year ago in her concession speech: the pain will be felt for a very, very long time, to *the last man standing*—man being used in generic sense and not gender sense

4

though the current POTUS is a male—Trump. I even hear promising and hopeful candidates are even assassinated, especially in the third world, not the kind of Gandhi mentioned elsewhere in this work. While jealousy too may not be ruled out, we cannot consider all the probable options in this particular case: there was a man Coker, the gubernatorial candidate of Peoples Democratic Party P D P in Lagos state, who news and opinion polls predicted would be the next governor of Lagos state in Nigeria who was murdered in his home before that election. Also to be mentioned was the assassination of a one-time presidential candidate and flag bearer of a major party who lost but his rival—the last man standing gave him the minister (secretary, the American call it) of justice: Chief Bola Ige, who was coldly murdered in his house in Ibadan when he came home briefly for the Christmas break from the capital Abuja on December 23, 2001. Shall we go on? No, we shall stop after mentioning an honorably discharged US Army officer, Moses, who traveled to Nigeria to vie for county president (local government chairman the office is called in Nigeria) who too was almost murdered but survived to return to the US where one of his hands was amputated in the Hines VA Hospital in the state of Illinois. No wonder some say, is it worth it to vie for office in Nigeria?

2.
The Human Mind and Emotions

The cognitive psychologists, according to Jerome Kagan and Ernest Havemann[1] think of the mind as possessing an executive function that makes comparisons and decisions. But our emotions deal with our feelings and motives. We are told that emotions are among the most powerful of forces that influence behavior. These boil up of their own accord, such as in an emergency when a child is seriously ill. A concerned mother who had always considered herself physically fragile finds that she can stay awake and alert for forty-eight hours. But in this game of politics how shall we consider the human mind and emotions? To do this we would need to classify the citizens into categories—at least two but there could be much more as in variations and mapping we see where a group merges into others but there could be several groups of people with regard to electioneering and campaigning. But broadly there are those that consider it a right and a duty to vote in an election, where I incidentally fall, and those, to mention two groups, that will not vote no matter what, and here we find the Jehovah's witnesses and some groups of nurses at the Cook County Hospital in Chicago where one said in a group I was present at, how does it concern me if anyone wins or loses?

I see that voting is not a sign of modernity or development of a people, and therefore requires *indoctrination* of people in all societies on how it is a patriotic duty and a sign of achieving an enviable government where the elected are accountable to the people. Did I hear a reader say, how so? Or how else could some still refuse not to vote and so have a say on how one's nation is governed? True, a single isolated vote is nothing, yet it is a truth we all have heard that little drops of water make the ocean. I don't need to have a friend or relation running for office before I vote. In fact, citizens register to vote before some people know they will be running or, should I say, before candidates declare their intention to run. Mind you, we are

7

talking about the human mind and emotions here in this chapter, and we have also said, those that are willing to vote and those that don't care can be boxed into two broad categories of which each could be further divided into smaller categories, but the group that don't care appear to have more categories within them. What brings these all together is that they don't give a damn about the democratic process and believe it or not, my father, Franklin O. Moore is one such man. So it shocked me to my bones in the 1970s as an undergraduate in the university when a senior in a different department but a friend told me a new party, the Nigerian Advanced Party (NAP), had been formed, and the founders included my father, Franklin Moore, and lawyer Tunji Braithwaite with their pictures and names on the front pages of leading newspapers. Not that we students generally bought newspapers in my time, but the vendors generally display their newspapers in the paths that students and lecturers pass through near motor backs on campus and pathways to lectures, and these display catchy topics of the day for enhanced sales. In the first instance, a lady did not know my father; she must just have taken a shot because I am Gregg Moore and the name she saw alongside Tunji Braithwaite's name was Franklin Moore, and besides that, party's registration and or declaration took place in Lagos where I was born and lived. By the way, this lady hails from Abakaliki in the southeast of Nigeria. The point I wish to make here is that if a psychic had told me a day earlier that my dad would join a political party I will tell him (her) to go to someone else and give their predictions. Here in America, I only hear on TV *California Psychic: the best or it's free. A dollar per minute*. The point I am making is that I don't think daddy even voted in elections or talked about politics, and here he was on the front page in a leading newspaper with Braithwaite and launching the Nigerian Advance Party (NAP)! That is what I mean by the central place of the human mind and emotions in our motivations for action. Even though I had not considered this previously, now as I write, I can imagine what happened. Lawyer Tunji Braithwaite had ambition to become Nigeria's next president at the time and maybe did some research on influencers of opinions in segments of Nigeria and must have found that daddy occupied a critical position in a segment of the nation that could provide a block of votes. How daddy agreed to join a party or form one with attorney Braithwaite still shocks me, but the point is made that we can change minds and work on emotions too for the good of society, and this thing we call democracy is the last hope of modern society, and we need to give it a trial.

But what is to be said about the religious group called the Jehovah's Witnesses? I think a good starting point is for incumbent executives, whether president or governor to locate professionals among them who are diligent and appoint one of them into a political office. This reminds me of what one head of state or president did in Nigeria a long time ago, meaning at least these Khaki boys listen to advice too, even though I am totally and completely against the military usurping power via coups and taking over the reins of power whether Jerry Rowling of Ghana, Charles Taylor of Liberia, Idi Amin of Uganda, or Gbadamosi Babangida of Nigeria. Yes, I am talking about the appointment of a unique man to a political office. Did you ever heard about Dr. Tai Solarin? He had a school where he was principal, a model high school in Ikenne, Nigeria, the Mayflower School. And there was a peculiar and queer man like him as one of his tutors teaching mathematics who too was a product of that Mayflower school but returned after obtaining a university degree in mathematics: the self-styled Brother William Kumuyi at the time but now pastor after abandoning teaching mathematics both in high school and also lecturing at the University of Lagos for his foremost passion, teaching the Bible—to now lead a megachurch, the Deeper Christian Life Bible Church. The two men had or have the same view about politics and democracy though one believes there is God and the other, I think, doesn't—either he thinks God is dead or that he doesn't know if there is a God, so he is an agnostic and not an atheist necessarily. Needless to say, at that time both principal and math tutor dressed alike but simple. Their dressing, however, changed in the same direction when a change occurred in both: one when he became the pastor of a megachurch and the other when he received a political appointment to become the chairman of the newly created bank at the time, the People's Bank of Nigeria, formed by a military president at the time! They both began to wear suits! We can change behavior towards democracy worldwide, and this should be the concern of all those that are already political and care about better order in our world. We should go for it not just for the money or even for money at all, but because democracy is for the greatest goods of the greatest amount of people, it could be said, since literarily defined, it is the government of the people by the people, and for the people!

3.
The Woman or the Man?

B y our question here, we intend to explore the notion whether there is a fundamental difference between the woman and the man in the occupation of certain leadership positions in existence in the human society—chiefly political, but we could talk too about other offices such as in business, academics, military, medicine, church (or may I add, mosque too, even though I am not an authority here), and you name it—any other subsection of the economy or society such as health care, family, etc. At the onset, before any analysis or reasoning, I say, no, there is no fundamental difference between the woman and the man in the occupation of certain leadership positions in existence in the human society but that of the family as the Creator of the family declared when the first family transgressed by eating the forbidding fruit. Now let us go and explore if this categorical exertion is true or if it be false.

We have today women boxers that we didn't have several years back. What about women in the military or as air pilots? The first time I discovered this was in grade school when the top students were not males or females but a combination of both sexes, and this continued to lead throughout our stay at that level, normally eight years, though some did it in seven in the Lagos Standard School system.

Again, in this work, we are concerned only about politics, and what is politics if not standing before a crowd giving speeches and thinking about how best to serve others—that is, being selfless and being able to withstand enticement, and also standing up for one's convictions? I think it includes diplomacy too and to be diplomatic is an act that can be learned by both sexes. Whereas the campaign trail can be really energy consuming, and we hear or read about women fainting on the campaign trail, men too have fainted or at least gotten exhausted. But thank goodness this is always for a limited time, and then things return to normal or the routine of governance. And has it not been said that a mother's heart is more tender and or loving? If this is true—and I think it is—this will almost make women better candidates for any office than men. Therefore, whatever assistance that is accorded to men in the political process, an equal amount if not even more, should be accorded the women too, especially as some describe them as the weaker sex. It should not be a sustainable reason, therefore, for women to leave the arena of politics to the men alone.

Whenever I consider campaigning and deception for a course (I almost said for a just course), the first thing that comes to mind is people and not a particular sex be they males or females. By people the reference is to candidates as well as the electorate. In the closing sentence of the introduction we read—*There is a superior advantage available only to the citizen-voter that is not available to all others anywhere*. This I say regarding the interview process and the selection of the best candidate for an open position. This will be easily understood by candidates who, in the past, have interviewed for managerial and or executive positions. This author has had the singular opportunity in interviewing for both but will only refer to one when he was interviewed for a signatory bank manager position for the Federal Reserve Bank of Nigeria, otherwise known as the Central Bank of Nigeria, in 1990 in the old capital of the Western Region of Nigeria at the Central Bank of Nigeria in Ibadan. A lot of preparation was done for this, and I drove long hours from the oil-rich city of Warri in Delta State where I was then employed as general manager of an oil servicing firm accompanied by MD who though was not at the interview with me. There was a panel of at least ten dignitaries who were all permitted by the chairman to ask questions of the candidates being interviewed, and we were not brought by groups—not even two candidates at a time appeared before this panel—and the interviews lasted for days! But one thing I discovered after getting onboard the managerial team of Nigeria's highest bank is that I most likely was more academically learned that some of interviewers for that very job. But it was I who had the goosebumps before the interview and not any of those who interviewed me!

In the same way, as citizen-voters we have the superior advantage of choosing who the next governor or president will be for our state and country, and no one has more right or power than you because we all have just one vote, which you can cast as you choose in a secret ballot, which, when added together determine the direction of the nation. To be frank, your decision or choice may be rejected by many others but elections still proves that you are a force to be reckoned with. For example, twice in a row when the American nation rejected my choice for who should be president of the United States, giving it to Barack Obama both times and rejecting John McCain and Mitt Romney! Any can imagine my joy when Trump was announced the forty-fifth president of the United States of America! By the way, Trump had not made the noble announcement that the US would recognize Jerusalem as the capital of Israel before he was elected president, nor could he have made it. It is therefore in your hands, citizen-voter, to determine which of the men or women will reign; do not take this privilege and responsibility lightly at all, and I think I can count on you.

4.
Some Actual Examples

Joshua 9:3-6: the inhabitants of Gibeon did work wilily, and went and made as if they had been ambassadors, and took old sacks upon their asses, and wine bottles, old, and rent, and bound up; And old shoes and clouted upon their feet, and old garments upon them; and all the bread of their provision was dry and moldy. And they went to Joshua unto the camp at Gilgal, and said unto him, and to the men of Israel, we be come from a far country: now therefore make ye a league with us. They got exactly what they wanted as the Israelite were fooled and this nation escaped the fierce massacre of the 7 nations the Hittites, Girgashites Amorites, Canaanites, Perizzites, Hivites and the Jesusites, that occupied the promised land before the arrival of the Israelites.

1 Samuel 21:10 ffl: And David arose, and fled that day for fear of Saul, and went to Achish the king of Gath. . . . And he changed his behavior before them, and feigned himself mad in their hands, and scrabbled on the doors of the gate, and let his spittle fall down upon his beard. Then said Achish unto his servants, Lo, ye see the man is mad: wherefore then have ye brought him to me? Have I need of mad men, that ye have brought this fellow to play the mad man in my presence? Shall this fellow come into my house?

David feigned madness but why should he when there may be no one on earth saner than him? That is politics; remember, he was the little boy who single handedly killed the Philistine giant Goliath, when nobody could face in in a fight, including army commander Saul, now hunting him to kill him.

2 Samuel 15:2–6: And Absalom rose up early, and stood beside the way of the gate: and it was so, that when any man that had a controversy came to the king for judgement, then Absalom called unto him, and said, Of what city art thou? And he said, Thy servant is of one of the tribes of Israel. And Absalom said unto him, See, thy

matters are good and right, but there is no man deputed of the king to hear thee. Absalom said moreover, Oh that I were made judge in the land, that every man which hath any suit or cause might come unto me, and I would do him justice! And it was so, that when any man came nigh to him to do him obeisance, he put forth his hand, took him, and kissed him. And on this manner did Absalom to all Israel that came to the king for judgment: so Absalom stole the hearts of the men of Israel.

And that political maneuver or tactic worked excellently for Prince Absolute that his father the King had to flee the capital ashamed and in fear, he and his followers.

Acts 23:2–5: And the high priest Ananias commanded them that stood by him to smite him on the mouth. Then said Paul unto him, God shall smite thee, thou whited wall: for sittest thou to judge me after the law, and commandest me to be smitten contrary to the law? And they that stood by said, Revilest thou God's high priest? Then said Paul, I wist not, brethren, that he was the high priest: for it is written, Thou shalt not speak evil of the ruler of thy people. And but that Paul saved his life from further accusation.

The tactics of politics may be used by any and all intelligent citizens, even by those who are so very far remote from politics, who are intelligent, for example the apostle Paul in the above passage. Paul's mission and goal was to please Almighty God and his Son Jesus Christ through the help of the Holy Ghost; moreover, he did not care if he died in the process of doing that. Yet at least twice in he dealt wilily one in the passage above, and the second below.

Acts 23:6–7: But when Paul perceived that one part were Sadducees, and the other Pharisees, he cried out in the council, Men and brethren, I am a Pharisee, the son of a Pharisee: of the hope and resurrection of the dead I am called in question. And when he had so said, there arose a dissension between the Pharisees and the Sadducees: and the multitude was divided.

Acts 24:26: And he hoped also that money should have been given him by Paul, that he might lose him: wherefore he sent for him the oftener, and communed with him.

Somebody tell me—did Paul not know that the governor wanted a bribe, and would it had been impossible for him to raise whatever amount from people that did not want Paul in jail in the first place? But who would have hoped that the highest paid individual around would be swayed by bribes or money? Why is a former governor in Illinois in jail now? Simply for saying, *what is in it for me* when a US senate seat was vacant in his state because the incumbent vacated that seat for a higher office, that of the POUSA, and it was on that governor's shoulder to fill it with a suitable replacement!

1 Kings 1:11–18–39 Wherefore Nathan spake unto Bathsheba the mother of Solomon, saying, Hast thou not heard that Adonijah the son of Haggith doth reign, and David our lord knoweth it not? Now therefore come, *let me*, I pray thee, *give thee counsel*, that thou mayest save thine own life, and the life of thy son Solomon. Go and get the in unto king David, and say unto him, Didst not thou, my lord, O king, swear unto thine handmaid, saying, Assuredly, Solomon thy son shall reign after me, and he shall sit upon my throne? Why then doth Adonijah reign? *Behold, while thou yet talkest there with the king, I also will come in after thee, and confirm thy words.* And Bathsheba went in unto the king into the chamber: and the king was very old; and Abishag the Shunammite ministered unto the king. And Bathsheba bowed, and did obeisance unto the king. And the king said, What wouldest thou? And she said unto him, *My lord, thou swarest by the LORD thy God unto thine handmaid, saying, Assuredly Solomon thy son shall reign after me, and shall sit upon my throne.* And now, behold, Adonijah reigneth; and now, my lord the king, thou knowest it not. And . . . thou, my lord O king, the eyes of all Israel are upon thee, that thou shouldest tell them who shall sit on the throne of my lord the king after him. Otherwise it shall come to pass, when my lord the king shall sleep with his fathers, that I and my son Solomon shall be counted offenders. *And, lo, while she yet talked with the king, Nathan the prophet also came in.* And they told the king, saying, Behold Nathan the prophet. And when he was come in before the king, he bowed himself before the king with his face to the ground. And Bathan said, My lord, O king, hast thou said, Adonijah shall reign after me, and he shall sit upon my throne? For he is gone down this day, and hath slain oxen . . . ; and, behold, they eat and drink before him, and say, God save king Adonijah. But me, even me thy servant, and Zadok the priest, and Benaiah the son of Jehoiada, and thy servant Solomon, hath he not called. Is this thing done by my lord the king, and thou has not showed it unto thy servant, who should sit on the throne of my lord the king after him? Then king David answered and said, Call me Bathsheba . . . And the king

sware, and said, As the Lord liveth, that hath redeemed my soul out of all distress, Even as I sware unto thee (Bathsheba) by the LORD God of Israel, saying, Assuredly Solomon thy son shall reign after me, and he shall sit upon my throne in my stead; even so will I certainly do this day. Then Bathsheba bowed . . . And the king said, Call me Zadok the priest, and Nathan the prophet, and Benaiah the son of Jehoiada. And they came before the king . . . And . . . the priest . . . anointed Solomon. And they blew the trumpet; *and all the people said, God save king Solomon.*

And so by the gerrymandering of a clergy, he orchestrated the successor to the greatest King on earth.

1 Kings 12:7 And they spake unto him, saying, if thou wilt be a servant unto this people this day, and will serve them, and answer them, and speak good words to them, then they will be thy servants forever.

This was the political advice given to the successor son of Solomon that he rejected outright and so lost the privilege to reign over the whole of the nation of Israel, which his father and grandfather enjoyed. This was, of course, of the Lord to confirm the word of prophesy of Ahijah the Shilonite which he spake to Jeroboam even while Rehoboam's father: Solomon was still the reigning monarch, because of his many sins which, unfortunately, is the true forecast of many if not all politicians.

We must consider one more passage of actual examples because of its relevance to America and may be moreso to Nigeria. And this is the passage:

I make a decree, That in every dominion of my kingdom men tremble and fear before the God of Daniel: for he is the living God, and steadfast forever, and his kingdom that which shall not be destroyed, and his dominion shall be even unto the end. He delivereth and rescueth, and he worketh signs and wonders in heaven and in earth, who hath delivered Daniel from the power of the lions (Daniel 6: 26–27, KJV).

This statement was made by no less a world political leader than Darius, who quelled the Babylonian Kingdom of Nebuchadnezzar and his descendants; you will remember that Nebuchadnezzar was the greatest concerning him the following was said:

It is thou, O king, that art grown and become strong: for thy greatness is grown, and reacheth unto heaven, and thy dominion to the end of the earth (Daniel 4:22).

Elsewhere it was said of this monarch: *Thou, o king, art a king of kings: For the God of heaven hath given thee a kingdom, power, and strength, and glory. And whosesoever the children of the children of men dwell, the beasts of the field and the fowls of heaven hath he given into thine hand, and hath made thee ruler over them all . . .* (Daniel 2:36—37). It was further said of Nebuchadnezzar, *The most high God gave Nebuchadnezzar thy father a kingdom, and majesty, and glory, and honor: And for the majesty that he gave him, all people, nations, and languages, trembled and feared before him: whom he would he slew; and whom he would he kept alive; and whom he would he set up; and whom he would he put down* (Daniel 5:18—19).

Yes, this man Nebuchadnezzar was great but Darius was even greater, and it is to his utterance that this section deals. Especially if we realize that the American totally forbid the mixing of religion with politics. One can almost say, next to jailing a politician that steals money, anyone that mixes politics with religion is next in line to go to jail. But at the time of writing I cannot lay my finger on such religious mixing, though there are ample cases of the Americans jailing religious preachers that mix their religion with something else. The case of the then flamboyant minister, the Reverend Jim Baker and husband to Tammy Faye Baker quickly comes to mind; he was summarily found guilty and sentenced to a jail time! I can go on but that will suffice. And so what will America say about a politician or president that would speak like Darius? I guess liberal America will say nothing, for it was a miracle for Daniel to be still alive the next morning after being thrown alive into a lion's den the previous day! Some may forget and maybe don't even know that of the two men—the sentenced and the sentencer—it was Darius the king that couldn't sleep but Daniel, the erstwhile prime minister and now a sentenced criminal slept like a baby. So religion can be mixed with politics after all when there is a miracle. That being so, Americans still will not permit Billy Graham to hold evangelic crusades if he were to run for the office of the president and emerge the last man standing. Instead they will expect him to talk budgeting, fiscal policy, and war in Iraq, certainly not holding a Bible in the stadium and or closing his eyes to pray long or even short prayers.

The above being the case, what should be said about a group of people called the Fulani's in Nigeria, who, according to history, were not even originally Nigerians like the Hausas of northern Nigeria. But now they want to run down the whole of Nigeria in the name of religion when their real motive is purely political and not religious at all. For I hear the Hausas where even already Muslims before the Fulani came and overran them, carrying out the bidding of Usman Dan Fodio, their ancestor. This, it is said, will not rest until their flag is installed in the Gulf of Guinea—a section of the Atlantic Ocean bordering the southern end of Nigeria. This, I hear, brings Fulani from all over Africa during the census to swell their population and so have the giant share of Nigerian resources together with the office of the president since democracy is nothing more than a game of numbers. Though what was believed to swell the northern population in Nigerian census I think is attributed to Purdah system of the Muslim faith where women cover their faces from men and may be strangers too apart from their husbands—so that a single female could be counted in a census on multiple occasions, maybe up to ten times since the census officer does not see the faces of those being counted in northern Nigeria. How then may this be speedily tackled and summarily dealt with as the political march to spread over the entire Nigerian nation and perpetually rule and govern by the Fulani people in the guise of religion we hear is progressing unabatedly? But there is still one similar example we should yet consider regarding the Russia collusion probe of the White House conducted by Robert Mueller, and the passage of choice is Jeremiah 38:24–26 Then said [President] Zedekiah unto [Advisor] Jeremiah, Let no man know of these words, and thou shall not die. But if the princes [congress, opposition and or the liberal press] hear that I have talked with thee, and come unto thee, and say unto thee, *Declare unto us now what thou has said unto the king [president], hide it not from us,* and we will not put thee to death; *also what the king [president]said unto thee:* Then thou shall say unto them, I presented my supplication before the king (or president), that he would not cause me to return to Jonathan's house (the prison), to die there.

This is like the Robert Mueller probe again and the forcing of the president's inner circle into confessions and plea deals. Is *In God We*

Trust still the American motto? I hope so. On the highlights of the probe, do people consider it wrong that the POTUSA cannot discuss some things with his immediate staff and require that they keep it completely secret? I did not quote from a tabloid but from the very word of God. One is almost sure that if Trump had made his decision to recognize Jerusalem as the eternal capital of Israel, the debate on that one topic would have snuffed out life from that glorious idea.

5.
What People Want: To Be Ruled or to Be Free?

I n a democracy, what really do people want? Choosing between being ruled or being free, it would appear people, that is, citizens, want to be free. However, a cursory look at happenings in various societies around the world appears to support neither. True, many, if not all, have agreed that democracy is the last home of modern man to produce a just society, and it has come to stay, and to the bulk of these millions, mere acceptance of democracy as a system is where their involvement begins and ends. A majority of people are more concerned about their respective jobs and maybe their leisure too, but certainly not politics or even registering to vote, and if we don't register, how then can we vote on Election Day? They are not concerned with who wins or loses, and therefore these citizens are not concerned with holding elected officials accountable. On a personal note, I do not think this is good enough. A day after Labor Day 2017 in America, I heard an African-born American say on *NCIS* that in Liberia, *we give the country to the weak and the fraudulent*. This is both true and sad, especially since Liberians do not intentionally or consciously give, but they shirk their duty to vote and by default give the nation to the weak and the fraudulent.

In reality, to be free and to be ruled are compatible, and that is exactly what democracy is all about. We are free when we are governed by duly elected officials who see themselves accountable to the electorate, the voting public, or the citizenry. Democracy is unique, different, and higher than any other form of governance. Just two example will do here—governance in the ivory tower—the *universities* and that by *a despot*. In the first, even though it appears really free, how many people hold degrees in any nation? Worse still, how many hold a PhD or have written enough papers to have earned the title of Professor? Besides, their world is an artificial world no matter how much the attempt to make it like real life and not the artificial set up it truly is. They have hospitals, markets, churches, offices, schools, police or security service, sports arenas, cinema, swimming pools, etc. but do they have a cemetery? No, and I can go on but the point being made here is that not all citizens of any nation can decide to go and reside permanently in a university. What about the other example of dictatorship? That by far is the worst form of government in the whole world, and therefore even worse than socialism and communism where the state thinks for and or decides for the citizenry, and so freedom is imprisoned. And when some, through one way or another, are afforded the opportunity to get out of the four walls of such countries, they chose not to return again, just like the fear prevalent in North Korea regarding the coming Olympics in South Korea that athletes who go for the games may not return back to their country after the game but will defect.

Another point that may justifiably be raised here could be related to happenings in the United States of America right now relating to the people's choice for president: Donald J. Trump. Which powerful interests did not support or want him? A recently written book: *Fire and Fury: Inside the Trump White House*² by Michael Wolff. There is also the talk of impeachment and or pressure to resign, which should not arise at all, since democracy should not be run by the rich and mighty but by the majority. Ask if the really rich should be permitted to run for public office, as these could hardly be called public servants but masters. Even then it will not be pure democracy when a section of the population is prevented from running for (any) office. The ballot box is and should always be the decision maker, not legislation about who can run and therefore who can govern. In this respect I do advocate that in the requirement of who may run for the office of the president of the United States two words be removed— yes, be completely deleted: *naturally born.*

Human society should absolutely respect the principles of democracy as individuality motivated candidates debate in the political arena and vie for offices and let *we the people* decide who governs. There are many ways—some really unethical—to truncate a candidate's ambition for office before election day, which this work will not go into even though it is totally and completely against these, such as bribing voters to vote in one way or another. But after a candidate has emerged—the last (wo)man standing—and barring some serious missteps like abuse of office, these should be allowed to run their terms as they later face opposition in another four years—even two or six years—years depending on the office in question. And what people want should be what the people want and not what disgruntled losers want no matter how high ranking they or their families may be in the society. I speak about the trouble some are giving to President Trump for no just cause and wasting public funds. These very people had prepared to laugh at him and scorn him should he have lost, but now that he won to become the last man standing, these same people will not rest. And if these do not take time, Trump will have another term after the 2020 election year, which I say though I am not a prophet.

6.
Comparing Democracy with Monarchy or Dictatorship

W hereas I do not think there is anything wrong with a monar-
chical government except that it is for a select few, whether
one considers the candidates or the kingmakers. And come to think of
it, politics is for a "select" few too when compared to the electorate,
which is everybody eighteen years and above.

But there is everything bad and nothing good at all about dictatorship! Though it is hard to draw the line around who is a dictator
and who is not, there are some examples: General Sani Abacha of
Nigeria, who is now deceased; General Ibrahim Babangida, also a
Nigerian who is yet alive; General Idi Amin of Uganda, also deceased
and permit me to mention two more: Adolf Hitler of Germany, who
slaughtered the Jews; and Napoleon Bonaparte of France, who had
to flee his country for his wickedness when nemesis was about to
catch up with him. Dictators may be animals in human skin at the
worst, or should we rather classify them as masters who choose to
be primitive and or blind to what is happening around them in the
world. Maybe most slave masters could be seen as dictators too. Just
as slavery was concertedly stopped worldwide, so should the world
come together and put out dictatorships wherever these may still
exist anywhere in the world, whether by rulers in military uniforms
or those in civilian attire. But how does dictatorship arise in any
society, it may be asked? We hear that power corrupts, and absolute
power corrupts absolutely. Every decent and right-thinking man or
woman knows that no one has it all or knows it all, and that is the
more reason why some occupy the position of advisers even though
we have seen some that sought advice and afterwards did contrary
to the inestimable advice offered to them, such as the Fourth King
[President]) of Israel—Rehoboam. Yet that was a very special case

for we read, "Wherefore the king hearkened not unto the people, for the cause was from the LORD, that he might perform his saying, which the LORD spake by Ahija the Shilonite unto Jeroboam the son of Nebat."[3]

It appears, however, that democracy could be successfully mixed up with monarchy—an experience that has done very well in Great Britain even though the Americans do not want any such mixtures in their country, which is understandable as the Pilgrims Fathers, another name for the founders of the United States of America, actually fled England due to alleged persecution from the aristocracy, the church, and the monarchy. But how is this mixture in African countries, taking Nigeria as an example? The situation is very fluid and amorphous with so many traditional rulers but I think it can be improved when a ruling house is obtained from each of the six geographical regions with each producing the queen or king of Nigeria in rotation that could be arrived at by a simple mathematical formula, only that the tenure of the king or queen would not be for, say, four years, as is done in the United States but for life, as is the case in monarchy.

7.
Limitation of Democracy

rrespective of how good a person and or system may be, we talk of shortcomings and or limitations of these and so what can be advanced as limitations of world democracies, or could they indeed be perfect? I suppose that since man by and large is not perfect, democracies too might not really be perfect, but I think some perfect men have tread this earth before who were at the helms of affairs of nations, and these were perfect even though these categories of perfect men are not very many. As an example, this writer puts forward the foreign governor Joseph, son of Jacob in the land or nation of Egypt at a time in history. But Joseph was not the only one in government in ages past that was perfect. Even with a perfect governor, there would be chains of command down the ladder with lieutenant or deputy governors and so on, even to the foreman. But the function of the head is leading by example, whatsoever that example might be. He or she does not need to tell the people what he is doing but *"a city set upon the hill,"* it has ben said *"cannot be hidden."* But in actual fact it is not always the best or most qualified candidate that gets elected, which in turn boils down to an imperfect and confused electorate. For should the general population be thinking right, which ought to be the case, these by and large will see through the gimmicks and displays of contending factions and candidates and choose the very best for whatever position is at stake. What about the peculiarities of office—or should we call this the temptations of office? Actually there are much more appropriate titles for what we are trying to say here, but the point should be clear that while in office, there are some that will get to the leader, may be even before his election, who will have ulterior motives that may not be as noble as the leader's especially while (s)he was a candidate. What then should be the attitude of the good leader to some of this? Influencers or effectors of governance may be contractors or even carrier employees or those lower down such as clerks, messengers, and maybe those in between. And what should we say about ethnic voting, that is voting for a candidate that is from one's ethnic region? Could this be possibly linked to the cry for the extinct nation of Biafra? As a section of the Nigerian nation thinks rightly or wrongly that other regions of the nation will not be for an Igbo candidate who may be running for the highest office of the land and so wrongly or rightly it is being forecasted that an Igbo president will never emerge in the nation Nigeria. But since politics is a game of numbers, is it possible for the Igbo citizens of Nigeria to embark on a massive drive of population increase via procreation and intertribal marriages of the male gender to other citizens of other regions of Nigeria? Though these two points appear against the core of the belief of the Igbo people: to have excessively large family and or diffuse their gene pool. This attack on the democracy appears not to lie with the Igbos alone but also with the Hausas and Yoruba too, the three largest ethnic groups in Nigeria.

The goal of democracy, however, is that the best candidate be elected as only heads are counted and not blood or race, all therefore having one vote each. But where will the lesson come from that you vote not for your kinsman necessarily but for the best of any category of candidates for an office? This also occurred here in America a short while ago, when a candidate that wasn't black labeled himself black to get the black votes, though indeed he was not white either, but from the other[4] race, which is neither white nor black! I remember clearly how a black female voter in the dead of the night on a busy junction of rail and road traffic in Chicago called on fellow blacks to help beat up a black wearing a T–shirt of a white presidential candidate of the rival party for daring to do so. The story did not end or start there, for earlier at that same Damien-Milwaukee-North Avenue junction in Chicago, a white gentleman seeing that same black campaigner concluded as he walked across North Avenue to pick a North Avenue bus from the Blue Line train that this (black) guy must be paid big to do that (wearing a vest with a white presidential candidate boldly displayed. This I say is a limitation of democracy as in the above narrated incidents only the black voter-campaigner was truly liberated.

8.
The Place of Money

C an somebody please permit me to say, the most important thing in life is money? And equally true is the fact that those *that go after money above anything else are the most foolish people on earth*. Maybe someone disagrees with that, but just one example and we shall move on. Somebody was permitted to ask for anything he wanted and he responded accordingly, that is, he asked for something he thought or felt he wanted above all others. The person that gave that blank check was surprised, or, should I say, even shocked, so he said because you have not asked for A, B, C . . . but have asked of Y, Z what people wouldn't ask for normally, I give you all these from A . . . even to X, Y, and Z! That encounter occurred between the newly coroneted King Solomon and God Almighty; and Solomon was deemed the wisest man on earth and was fabulously rich too even though he did not go after money first above all other things. Do you, my readers, now agree with me *that those who go after money above anything else are the most foolish people on earth*? Money is so very important in the democratic process that its place can never be adequately accounted for or comprehended. What really can be done without money, it may be asked? Well maybe there are many things it could advance. How then may we continue? With the answer, through the use of volunteers! But are volunteers actually free and devoid of money underpinnings? While this may be partially so, there are certain things that the use of money must come to play. Actually when a person is classified as a volunteer, the primary definition is that the person does the assignment pro bono, but should that also exclude transportation expenses and lunch too? Of course not, or else these ought to be classified as donors to the cause and not volunteers. So what do we need money for in electioneering? Many things, or everything! I write to make a distinction between what money is needed for and how it should be obtained. Some years ago during the ninety-day period of petition signing, acting as a circular for self, I came across a white female who, on requesting her endorsement or signature, asked me only one question after listening to me: will you send me emails after giving you my information? Oh no, I said but mind you her concern was genuine, for she saw I was a prospective candidate wanting to get on the ballot to run. Yet she remembered somewhere in her mind that politicians send emails indiscriminately to ask for donations from names that they came across somewhere or somehow. But actually the information on the petition sheets are not for the circulators and neither are they for the candidates they represent but only for the electoral board that will determine if the candidate has enough support from the citizens to compete for an elected office. So while endorsers' information sure helps a candidate gets on the ballot, they are not to scrutinize these list in order to ask for funds or anything, for that matter, not even for campaign help, as this will occur later in the open and should that endorser buy what that candidate wants to sell above all others, he is sure to vote for him or her on election day. But this endorsement thing is very crucial I think. For after that, the candidates are on their own to make or break themselves. Just help them on. But this chapter is about the place of money in the electioneering process.

First the candidate should have some money to begin with or find it somehow. I hear it said that Bill Clinton even before becoming governor of a state, not even the president of the nation, asked for a loan from an uncle I think not sure now, who was generous and helped him. Bill asked an uncle, not the general public, for a startup donation. But seriously, no candidate should ask for—or is it needs—the citizen's money but instead should ask for their votes. Should any disagree with this logic, imagine two candidates, A and B, with one getting a dollar each from every voter before election and the other getting one vote each from every voter on election day. Who is the worse off and who is the better off? I guess responses to this question will vary, and any side could win, but as for me, the choice is clear. It is the vote the candidate needs and not the voters' dollars or even nickels.

And talking about money, does anyone remember the dirty linens being washed in public of two very rich presidential aspirants in the last US presidential election in the first year in office of the wining candidate, precisely around the month of November 2017. Who is more corrupt: Hilary or Donald, it may be asked. Maybe both, one, or neither. But talking about proposed bribes to the tune of millions of dollars to a US army general, whether true or not, reminds one of an African adage: *Isale Oro O legbin* literally translated *the foundation of wealth is messy.*

9.
Motivations for Aspiration

S omewhere in this work we said someone, a Canadian, defined politics as the activity that destroys the last hope of life and society. At some other time at the Union Station, while a candidate was attempting to garner signatures during the midterm elections so as to be on the ballot the next November, a suburban voter who graciously signed the nomination sheet did not just stop there but went on the ask the circulator/candidate, "Do you too want to go to jail?" He simply responded, "No I would not." You may then ask, why such a question? Should that would-be endorser not just refuse to endorse or endorse and wish the candidate good luck either inwardly or verbally?

Of course, both understand each other or at least the question asked and the answer offered. Two previous governors of that very state or maybe more were thrown into jail after they were tried to serve some prison time while in office for deeds done against the state and contrary to the law of the land. It need not be said that the allegations against both ex-governors for which they were innocent until proven guilty had to do with fraud and or embezzlement. Money is a magnet, one might say, but should that then be a motivation for some, many, or all to go into politics? Sincerely I think money shouldn't be a motivation for running for an elected office, but as things are, it seems to be a very big factor. Yes, why we go into any profession is to have money for the upkeep of ourselves and families, but there ought to be the service reason too. It is just that the mode of service through politics is different. For other jobs, the individual goes to school and acquires training in specific areas, applies for job opening in that area, and then goes before a panel of two or three— maybe up to seven or as few as one and is interviewed for the job in private. But not so with securing an elected office. Here everybody has a say, and an equal say of a vote each and the minimum academic qualification is not much at all, just a high school diploma.

But for a politician to be successful in office, not just to be successful in an election as so be the last man standing, (s)he ought to have real motivation for doing so. It could be seeing people not doing it right on being elected and wanting to make a difference by showing the world how to serve. It could be just seeing how brilliantly a candidate performs in campaigns and debates regarding how poorly others did as indeed occurred to this author in his first year in the university when he was not even qualified to vote. In this regard I want to give honor to a student, Dele Babatunde, of the University of Ife in the 1970s. I have not seen him since graduation and may never see him, but his demeanor and oration during speeches, debates, and interviews sure motivated. Well, it is not enough to be motivated to run for office; you must have a tangible agenda or program to better the lives of the people you are elected to serve. Returning to Dele Babatunde: the one-time student union president of the University of Ife, now Obafemi Awolowo University in Ile-Ife, Nigeria, he and his colleagues in other campuses throughout the nation of Nigeria caused an all-encompassing strike that all universities were closed down while clamoring for the removal of the Secretary (Minister, he is called in Nigeria) of Education: *Alli Must Go*. They achieved their aim: Dr. Ahmadju Alli, a medical doctor, was removed from office, but must university students cause so many disturbances in a nation or strike at all? Maybe that is a question for another discussion, not here. But a good government will ensure that it meets the yearning of its subjects or at least be seen to be doing so. I sure wish to serve.

10.
One or Two Things That Are the Most Important Requirements of Aspirants

T here are books that discuss this point elaborately for the aspirants attempting to aid them in achieving their goals, but that task is not what this chapter is all about. Here we are concerned about the people to be governed so that these may have a peaceable and prosperous time. It is not to say, however, that candidates will not find this chapter useful as it could dissuade a would-be candidate from further pursuing his or her political dream should she discover that she does not actually have what it takes to be in office, especially if they have consciences because it appears so many politicians don't have consciences at all. While some discarded them before coming into office, others, it appears, lost their consciences while in office. By others this writer does not mean all others, just some others, since some politicians go in with their consciences remain in office with them, and they also exit whole with their moral self intact. So what are one or two things the electorate should look for in candidates, which if not in them, they should be written off completely, immediately?

In discussing this I know we all have points that are crucial to us, and so for a moment, can the reader please put down this book and sit back to consider the question, *What one or two things are most important requirements of aspirants?* Then read on. One is not given to the love of money or lack of contentment. If to any degree the would-be candidate is deficient in these, he should not go into politics, but if he does, should have just one vote, his alone and not even that of his wife or husband or of their children that are eighteen and above. There is so much to say about going to politics for money or lacking contentment or being greedy but no time to say that here.

Suffice it to say that for some it can be said, *for a penny that person can be sold (or bought)*. But there is another thing I should mention here though there are many more that we could consider together. Is the person qualified to lead? And by that I do not mean age or possession of a high school diploma since those are already clearly spelled out for each office. Qualifications have multiple dimensions including ability to face the heat from the governed, be they supporters that did so in this first instance for anticipated favors that may be contrary to the law of the land. It also includes coping with blackmail from detractors and other enemies existing or suddenly aroused due to your new office. Should qualifications not include a good heart and fairness to all? I think they should, for a vindictive person is not worthy to be entrusted to a public office of any magnitude or order, especially of that of a president. I hear Donald Trump loves loyalty. That in itself may not be bad, but loyalty at all cost could be really dangerous and bad except in one area alone, which is within the bond of marriage. However, many seem not to know this at all, and so divorce thrives everywhere and on all continents of the world. What a shame. Again that is not exactly the subject matter of this book, so just mentioning that is sufficient. This may be hard to state in writing, yet I will venture into it.

Talking about the one or two things that are most important requirements of aspirants so as to determine who to support or vote for, a case comes to mind sometime in the last century during the presidential election season of a nation. Two of the candidates were very well known to this author, and they both have sterling attributes. For example, they are both great orators in their own right. As for one, when he speaks you might think you are intoxicated or that a dead body nearby could resurrect just listening to him. The other speaks pure Queen's English and there is no one like him. Incidentally both of them attended the same university, the best in the nation, and also the premier university manufactured from London itself, and both took the same courses while on campus—I'm not sure now which graduated first, but I can guess they were there together at some point. After graduation one branch off to study law while the other branched into finance and banking. The commonest title of one was deacon while that of the other was chief though they both held the chieftaincy title from their various states and counties (local government areas). Actually the one that using the chieftaincy title could have been a deacon too had he belonged to the Southern Baptist Convention, which is American. But he pitched his tent just like this author's grandfather, Sir William Moore, with the Church of England that may not have the deacon title but maybe that of elder instead, the highest a layman can attain in their respective denominations. And I have heard both preach before, and when you hear them you would think they both received their messages from almighty God directly. I forgot to mention that at the university they were both members of the Student Christian Movement, SCM, an international organization that the late Chief Akano Ibiam and Elder Ejiwunmi independently exported to South East and South West Nigeria respectively. I can go on but, let me sum up. Both wanted to run for Nigeria's president at the same time, Deacon Gamaliel Onosode and Chief Bola Ige. Who, then, should one vote for? We are considering electing the right man for the right job. True, Ige had been in politics for long serving as state governor, and Onosode had not been, but does that disqualify him? What about David, who singlehandedly defeated the giant when the equivalent of a general, major generals, and other high ranking army officers were in the battlefront, like Saul, Eliab, and Jonathan, but none could volunteer to face Goliath in a duel? How do you choose between two very great candidates? Well none of these two won the presidency. Even one did not even clinch his party's ticket! So I ask again, what one or two things are most important requirements of aspirants? I did not have a problem in choosing between the deacon and the chief regarding who should be the Nigeria's next president. I actually went to one of these two men even before either declared their intention to run. Though I feared I might not be granted access, having not previously booked an appointed, when my name was mentioned to the man who happened to be in at the time of my visit, he instructed that I should be let in, and the security guard took me upstairs to a dining table area where I was ushered to a seat. Within about five minutes or so the candidate came to meet me and after an exchange of pleasantry, I ask a question to introduce my mission. What would you want to run for I asked, and the candidate chief or deacon said to me, "*What the people want, that I will do.*" So I replied disappointingly, this was not what God told me before traveling across states to come see you. *God said you want to run for president, and He is going to help you.* Immediately the man changed mode and gave me his entire itinerary, the cities he would be at, when, and the respective venues of these meetings. I guess he accidentally mistook me for a journalist, or why would he give that type of answer to my question? But did I not mention to the gate man who I was? I sure did, but certainly not a journalist. So respectively I told him I would not go to any of those meetings but when he came to Lagos state, I would show up. So he gave me the hotel in Ikeja the Lagos state capital where his rally would take place and the date and time. But unfortunately, when he came to Lagos, I tried to see him in the hotel but was not allowed to, so I left.

As mentioned above none of these two godly men became president then. They are both now dead, and incidentally both in their respective homes: one on his bed after a brief illness—the Baptist deacon of the American Southern Baptist faith—but the other was murdered by still yet to be known hired killers when he came to his home in his city for the Christmas break. Though far way in the United States at the time of this gruesome act, the very next day I saw in my email inbox in the Chicago Northside that *the Chief and member of the Church of England died yesterday*. So I did not vote in that election because I was far away from Nigeria at the time, but I know who I would have voted for, should I have been in Nigeria, and most likely my one vote would not have changed the vote—the Baptist army general, who was once the head of state would still have won. I am not against the army, but I am sick that in Africa, they leave their duty of protecting their nation from external aggression and come meddle with what should be left for the courts and the police—the internal problems of the nation, which they do by staging a coup d'état. All soldiers that wish to run for any political office after leaving the army should openly declare that *I am against the coups that have taken place in this nation and say I am sorry and apologize for them.*

11.
Otibaje Tunshe: (There Is) Dislocation—Fix It

When the first habitat of man was prepared and ready for occupation, the Architect and Town Planner said it was very good, even though it was just a garden for two; a man and a woman with so many animals and flower trees! But with time as the human population increased and atrocities committed increased too, like the initial ones of murder, jealousy, fear, and complaint, there arose dislocation in the system, and ever since there has been a dire need to fix human society. By the way, some of these dislocations did not appear immediately, nor are they all caused by man like what would occur in Africa and around the world at that time.

The president of Egypt had dreams concerning future calamity but didn't give a hoot what the meaning of his dreams were. Forces beyond us humans affect and influence our world, yet it is our business to fix all these, including the distribution of resources, and possibly supervision even in the free world at least to ensure that men compete lawfully for the control and ownership of society's resources. The story of how a foreigner from Palestine saved Africa and the rest of the world from perishing is well knowwn when a prisoner came out of jail to solve a riddle and did not return to serve his full term, but instead became the governor of Egypt by a simple unanimous election result.

But the problem that faces the world today is more than hunger, even though hunger is one of the problems of the world if not even the most critical. The rich and the powerful even create more problems for the world like oil-rich Iraq and the threat of nuclear war. What about religious fanatics that will indiscriminately maim and kill those of other religions they term rival religions? And some governments— for example the Nigerian government—are powerless to handle the situations. Categories of citizens cannot tolerate each other within nation and so want to secede — again, Nigeria is an example with the Biafra war in the late 1960s, and surprisingly the cry for Biafra is still raising its ugly head in this age and time in a new century. Not to be forgotten is the civil war in the US when some slave owners in the South refused to stop slavery; after that Abraham Lincoln abolished it, and so these were made to stop by the force of war, which they almost won and could have succeeded. We know so many things are dislocated and out of joint in our world. These all need to be fixed and included are: robbery of all kinds and also drug trafficking and child trafficking. What about gang violence? All these are the reasons why we need good governments around the whole wide world so that the people may lead peaceable and prosperous lives.

By their determination and action to run for office, elected public servants take it upon themselves — unlike those in the private sector, even though these too ought to show social responsibility — to fix dislocations in the system and not just aspire for and go into office to loot the system or at least just please themselves or work minimally without due regard for what is the greatest good for the greatest number of people. Those that think the goal of public officers is to amass wealth should really be jailed and not go scot-free at all. The US has set a good example but so many countries in Africa are still in the dark ages regarding this single crime of looting the public treasury to foreign bank accounts in Switzerland, the United States, and name it, but still go scot-free. It must stop now. Politicians should mend dislocations in the system and not widen the cracks they met on assumption of office, and those that will not do this should be made to return the money looted and also sent to jail.

12.
The Least You Can Do

D emocracy, we have been told, is a government of the people, by the people, and for the people. If this really true, why then do so many people do absolutely nothing and so cause their society to be less than it can be or even in some cases to actually decay or rot away? Fortunately, or should we say unfortunately, this author has lived in two countries for scores of years. In one, for example, there is electricity supply **24 / 7**,and in the other the people experience black outs continuously for days if not weeks on end with the accompanying problems of noise and air pollution from generators, short life expectancies, sickness, and destruction of businesses that require power for refrigeration. But we can get rid of these problems by simply counting ourselves in, that is, as part of the society. Yes, the least you can do. Just yesterday the last day of October as today is Wednesday the 1st of November, 2017 while in a public transport, this writer witnessed something through the window and spoke aloud *that man should be jailed.* And immediately from the row behind another replied, *jailed for that?* And that was how the discussion ended.

It was on the Chicago Transit Authority—a CTA bus—and for a long stretch of the highway, repair work was being carried out with boards and tapes as barriers to prevent people from crossing over everywhere but only in designated areas. The laborers had closed for the day but the traffic was still bad on South Homan Avenue, south of the Chicago Avenue crossroad. So as this man stepped off the bus, he just walked past the cemented floor and did not even jump so that the cemented floor was marred exactly to the shape of the man's shoe and how hard he stepped on the wet cement. The laborers would come tomorrow and resume work further off from where they stopped, and when the already worked area is dried, the barricade would be removed and that dent will be there for ages and may even cause further cracks and dents. That was why this writer said that man should be jailed as another retorted: *for that?* My challenger definitely did not see that action as wanton destruction of public property, maybe because it fell within the scope of *unintended consequences of human actions*. I am sure if people were deliberately breaking, burning, or looting properties, private or public and he hears such utterance, he would not have said, *for that?*

Nations of the world can improve and get better if we do just a little, every one of us. And for our context here all ages eighteen and above ought to register to vote, obtain a voter's card, and vote on election date no matter what. And by so doing, especially because people want the best, the better candidate will be elected even if a fraction of the voting public allow other mundane sentiments to determine their voting behavior. That man *yesterday* at Homan and Ohio that destroyed the good job of the city department of transportation most likely will not vote on election day even if he has a voter's card, and if he votes, will not care to vote for the better candidate, since he does not even know the better thing to do when the police are not there watching him.

But certainly to get the right candidates into office there are many things we can do even to encourage them along the way as these struggle to provide superior service to the people, which we all know and want, but my concern here is just the least you can do— hear the candidates speak, and read about them. The easiest though is watching them on TV, but above all listen to your heart. But first you must cultivate a good heart, and cultivating a good heart is not our concern here. But am sure you know how to do that, even if it is hard.

Is it proper in this chapter of *the least you can do* to also mention the greatest you can do? Maybe I should, and actually there are three greatest things you can do or maybe four, and these I want to address these right now, so get ready. Topping the least is voting on election day. In the last US presidential election, there were may be at least four candidates, but the press would want you to believe there were just two. Actually generally you may not know about other candidates until you get into the polling booth—electronic or mechanical—to cast your vote and back luck for the write-in candidates because they will be invisible at the polls. Let's go back four years from the 2016 US presidential election, which again the media made me believe only two candidates were running: millionaire Mitt Romney, and then there was the people's choice, incumbent Barack

Obama. I was shocked to get to the polling booth to see at least two other names on the ballot. Well these did not concern me, so I voted and got out, even though MD came and canceled my vote by voting for the person I did not vote for, even though she too does not think it is right for a man to marry a man or a woman to also wed another woman—all the things Obama stood for. Yes, in the 2016 I made up my mind to be the very first person to get to my polling station and I was the first voter outside since the officials were already in who too might have voted before start time or do they do it after since during the official voting time, these have to be available to check the voters as authentic and sign them in to vote. Yes, I was the first to enter, but actually I was not the first to submit my ballot sheet as I took my time to decide who I wanted to vote for in all the other positions using my own formula or criteria for apart from the presidency, which I had no formula or criteria for but to just do what the party says: voting for the man with the party ticket even though not everybody in the party agreed. For example the *Never Trump* movement. These should have removed the first letter on to read *Ever Trump*, but that is not our concern here now. Just vote on election day or earlier should your country have early voting like the United States of America.

The second thing in the order of importance is to sign a petition for someone to run. Just yesterday, exactly a year to midterm election I signed my first petition. I was on the CTA, and a woman came up with a clipboard and sheets, talked timidly, walked past me, and went to sit down. I turned back and beckoned to her to come over, which she did, telling me how to do it: my signature first . . . then Chicago etc. So I told her I did not live in the city; she said, fine, but include your city, and I did while signing the petition. This circulator then gathered some energy and started approaching voters and obtaining some more signatures. She then got off way before my stop as I saw her walking across the bus path at a red light lighting a cigarette with a match! So if you can, sign a petition and help someone get on the ballot to contest. Mind you, signing a petition does not mean you must vote for that candidate. In my case on that day I did not know the office she was vying for or talk more to know her ideology—for example, whether she believes in gay marriage, for instance, or abortion, which the progressives call the woman's right to choose. We shall deal with that in campaign, not now. Just endorse a candidate, and let the competition be keener.

The third and I almost said the most important but cannot say that since I started from the most important is for you, my reader, to run. That is vying for office, but I know so many will not do for so many reasons. Once while vying for the office of county president abroad, called the chairman of a local government area, one of the leaders of thought in my area said, "You made politics so nice to participate in, I would have loved to compete too." Go for it, sir, I told this land-lord (or property owner) but he said, "I do not have a high school diploma!" So in that country, you cannot run for office without a high school diploma, called the first school-leaving certificate. Is it not in that very country or was it in another when another candidate was challenged that he did not possess the high school diploma—yet that candidate won the presidency of his country, an oil-rich country, the richest oil producing nation in its continent. So many people may not run, but the most and or least important thing any citizen can do and should do is vote! What really therefore is the least you can do to wrap it up. To make time to go vote your conscience for who you consider the best for that office and never miss another election after of course making sure your voter's registration is in place at least two months before an election. The list or most dignified is compete with the above first three: Gold, Silver and Bronze, but I want to mention one more thing and that is to run and then win, to be the last man standing like say, Donald J. Trump; you know many more like him: Nelson Mandela, Margret Thatcher, and Dr. Kwame Nkrumah.

13 Summary and Conclusion

What have we been discussing and what have you, dear reader, grasped from it all? There has been governance of societies all through the ages, some simple and some highly complex. This was not first simple and later very complex, for we have indeed had some complex governmental structures even a long time ago before this present modern-day structure. One thing is clear: the idea to be implemented could be stated in very simple terms but the mechanism of its implementation could be really cumbersome. But before we go into these so-called simple ideas, which may be cumbersome in implementation, we need to remember what this book is really all about, even though its subject matter is intricately woven to some processes which it therefore had to touch upon like *good governance* and *exemplary public service* that is top notch, though difficult to come by. We have been talking about democracy and politics and a specialized aspect of politics, and if you like a very tiny aspect of politics but nonetheless a very important segment of it: the *electioneering campaign* and the choosing of the right candidate. I mean right for the majority of any nation's citizenry since that is what democracy is all about, after all. Any governmental structure is beneficial for some people no matter how small, even if only to the despot or dictator and his cabal and or family. But that is not what democracy is all about, this form of governance that we have tried to establish as the last home of the common man.

Do people come with good intentions to govern and eventually fall by the wayside? Yes, of course, although we have also tried to establish that the majority of those that aspire to office, especially in the Third World, have no noble goals and instead wish to amass wealth for themselves and their cronies. We are not saying that greed is not exhibited by people in the First World, only that there are sanctions that are operative and effective. Taking two countries as examples, the United States of America and Nigeria: when has a Governor served his term in a state and shortly after that (s)he is tried and sent to jail for fraud and like offenses in these two countries? Maybe none in Nigeria, although it could be there are some that this writer does not know about. But not so in the US. Years back while attempting to run for the governorship of the State of Illinois in the Midwestern region of the United States of America, and while collecting signatures to be on the ballot as an independent candidate, somebody of another race signed the petition but first asked this writer who was gathering signatures at that time as a circulator within the ninety days allowed: Do you wish to go to jail? This he asked because governors have been thrown in jail after their tenure in office, and the last governor who served at the time convicted and in jail! The answer that circulator gave before that elector-voter signed his petition sheet may be irrelevant here, but he simply said: I will not go to jail for fraud. Sanctions should be enforceable and in place, but this cannot be when people don't know the real purpose of democracy and or politics, which some think is the sure way to loot public funds without repercussions. I have heard about a former state governor in Africa that is richer than seven states put together in his country and he walks around as a free citizen, even styled a king maker in subsequent elections either for that of governors, lower offices, or even president! Can that take place in America? I don't think so, and neither should it take place anywhere in the world: whether Third World, Second World, or even the First World.

Some unfortunately do not want to have anything to do with politics because of this. They have their counterparts in the developed world who also abstain from voting, albeit for entirely different reasons, and these are not helping matters. No nation is totally and completely corrupt—not even Sodom and Gomorrah, which were literally burnt down to ashes. All citizens of any nation should therefore by their individual and solitary actions see that the best of their generation get into political offices and fix the part of society that is broken and dislocated. We have had exemplary governors, rulers before in the past, and we can still have them again. That stranger, Joseph, in the nation of Egypt was an example, and there are some more everywhere, really. If voters will make a little effort to help get the best candidates into office by both mandatorily voting and doing a little extra that their conscience will dictate and not the appeals of the candidates—which could be anything. Therefore, it may not be proper to mention any such things at the end here other than to get *registered and vote*.

Yet some people still think their country is far gone and irredeemable and may not want to listen to any such arguments as presented in this writing. There are things I hear that may not be necessary to mention here. For example some think politics is a do-or-die affair! Are such candidates and their supporters actually coming to serve the people or do they have ulterior motives? It appears to so many that, going into politics is fulfilling ambition, not service, and fulfillment of ego or even accumulation of whatever such politicians wish to amass. But service is giving of oneself for fellow citizens whether locally or nationally. Therefore, both candidates and citizen-voters ought to seriously think it through before announcing their intention to run and before going to the polls on election day to pick the next occupier of the post being contested for which for all purposes could be the return of the incumbent or his or her ousting and the replacement with a fresh or new blood for the next four years. We all must realize and embrace the notion that it is only democracy that truly bring us all together as same and equal. Many people will certainly never become the Queen of England, the Sultan of Sokoto, Oba of Benin, OluBadan, or the Olu of Warri, and a new one: the Obi of Onitsha, but any of us could be the next governor, prime minister, or president since the former is by ascription and the latter by achievement via the electoral process. All therefore should get involved, and *all* means citizens eighteen years and above. I cannot wait to hear the result of the next elections in countries where this book, *Dislocation . . . (**Otibaje . . .**)*, will get to and be assimilated. The problem of this present world system is that there is too much that cries out for a solution that must be fixed. Your nation is waiting for a brand-new you to come into office and fix the system that is broken! But first you must scale through an honorable panel of judges, the interview board that is millions and not even thousands or the usual five to twelve in corporate interviews—the citizens-voters who hopefully will take their superior role of determining who gets elected to the various offices to be filled: whether councilor/alderman, chairman/mayor house of reps, senators, governors, or the nation's president. This dislocation must be fixed. Otibaje—Tunshe! Who therefore is the more important actor: the candidate or the voter? Of course the voter, but mind you, the candidate is not short-changed because he too is a voter with one vote just like any other citizen voter that is eighteen or over.

References:

[1] Jerome Kagan and Ernest Havemann, *Psychology: An Introduction* Third Edition, Harcourt Brace Jovanovich International Edition NY© 1972. Printed in the United States of America.

[2] Michael Wolff, *Fact and Fury: Inside the Trump White House,* Henry & Holt Co, Macmillan NY 2018.

[3] 1 Kings 12:15 Life *Application Bible* King James Version, Tyndale House Publishers Wheaton, Illinois USA © 1988.

[4] Gregg Moore, *White Black and Other*, Xulon Press, Florida USA © 2013.

Chief Obafemi Awolowo Dr. Nnamdi Azikiwe
Sir Abu-Bakr Tafawa Balewa